DROPS OF MORNING DEW

REFLECTING HOPE ANEW

JANE JONES

Copyright © Jane Jones
All Rights Reserved.

This book is dedicated to Mrs. Geraldine Ward,

who always was an immense support, inspiration and
encouragement to me.

Her wonderful legacy will always be remembered.

Contents

Contents

Foreword

As I breathtakingly went through Jane's book of poems, my thoughts strayed to a little girl, who I'd watched growing up. Did I see bits of her those years that would finally blossom into a poet? I think I did. A poet, doesn't have to reveal herself in verse, but rhyme and flow, and the grace of poetic form, can reveal itself in a myriad different ways, and I saw such: I had the blessed privilege of seeing Jane entering this world. As she grew, she amazed me with the varied talents she possessed: Her graceful playing of the piano, was poetry in motion, and so too the plaintive notes that flowed from her violin. I was awed as I saw that in every Olympiad she participated, she rose higher in rank.

Tragedy struck when Jane was still young, and her father was called home to glory but her mother continued to encourage and motivate Jane and her sister and her efforts paid off as the world soon saw that there was nothing impossible for Jane. She attempted everything headlong and made a success of it. And then poetry entered her life when at thirteen, her English teacher inspired her to write a poem. She tried her hand as she always did at everything, but this time her pen flowed into the stream of verse and stayed there. There was no turning back after that. She used poetic form to write on various subjects and for various occasions always focusing on the goodness, greatness and faithfulness of God.

I had the privilege of reading all her works and also the many music videos made by both her and her sister. God has blessed her with self- confidence and as she continues to reach for the stars, I wish her all the very best for all her future endeavours. May this book of verse make you, dear reader, see not just the glory of a living God but the heights He can lift all those who place their trust in Him, as Jane is doing!

Mr. Ruben Moses

Acknowledgements

I would like to thank all those who motivated and encouraged me throughout my journey of writing poetry so far. I thank my mother for supporting me in my every endeavour and my sister for believing in me and motivating me to be my best.

I would especially like to thank my English teacher, Anitha ma'am, without whom this book would never have existed. Thank you for helping me unearth this once hidden talent of writing poetry, for always inspiring and encouraging me, and for giving me the idea to publish my work. I'm ever grateful.

I wish to express my gratitude to Mr. Ruben Moses for writing the foreward for this book, and for all his support and encouragement.

I also thank you, dear reader, for taking the time to read these words of mine.

Preface

'Drops of Morning Dew' is my first collection of poems, written over a span of three years. These poems are inspired by various people, occasions and nature, and seek to find the light in every situation – the rainbow in every storm.

It's hard to believe that I once doubted my ability to write a poem, but once I tasted the beauty of expressing my thoughts and ideas in lines that rhyme and seem to speak for themselves, I never looked back. Following a definite rhyming scheme and maintaining a meter in each line has always been important to me while writing a poem, for it makes the words sound like musical notes.

Discovering the beauty of words, and weaving them together to unveil beautiful poems has truly been a wonderful and fascinating experience.

I hope that these poems will be, to your mind, like drops of morning dew – refreshing and filling you with hope anew.

1. How To Write A Poem

A poem – oh how beautiful!
Just simple words, yet how powerful!
It speaks to one in a soft whisper,
A door to another world, that fills one with wonder.

A poem, you say, oh why can't I?
Well, why don't you just give it a try?
The question then arises - but how?
Ask no more, let's begin now.

Well, you can write a poem
In the comfort of your home,
Or out in the bright sunshine,
Or in the stillness of the night.

Take a deep breath and relax
Just let your mind be fully lax,
While your imagination runs wild
And you dream like a little child.

Let your thoughts freely flow
E'en though at times it might be slow,
Just jot it all down on a sheet,
Don't bother if it's not neat.

Finding the right words is the key
Don't look for words too grand or swanky;
Use simple words to express your thoughts,
For little words do mean a lot.

And also try to think about words that rhyme,
But don't get worked up, just take it one step at a time.
Don't have any restraints, just let yourself go,
You'll be surprised at how the words just flow.

After a while, try some figures of speech,
For they really do have the power to outreach;
There's personification, always ready to lend a helping hand;
While simile, like salt, makes sure things aren't too bland.

Metaphor is a root that goes down into the depths,
And alliteration, sounds almost alike altogether give a little zest;
And repetition – using words, again and again
Are all powerful tools that ensure your words are not in vain.

The most important thing you must always keep in mind,
Is to have no boundaries, and let nothing be defined;
E'en though it might not be great in everyone else's sight,
Be true to yourself, while you think and while you write.

And you'll discover the beauty of writing a poem, wherein,
Words just take shape as your thoughts flow out from within;
Always be yourself, never fail to be true:
For the best poems that you write are the ones that show you.

PONDERING LIFE

2. Piece by Piece

I emptied out the thousand pieces of a puzzle,
Awestruck at how they all were so different;
Overwhelmed at the thought of putting them together,
Wondering if I'd ever figure out where each one went —
But I earnestly began sorting it out, piece by piece.

As I slowly began putting the pieces together,
'Twas striking how each one had its own special place;
For sometimes it seemed that another piece looked right,
But no, there was a unique piece meant to fill that space —
And so I started unravelling it, piece by piece.

And one day, devastated, I almost gave up,
For the wind had made of my hard work a huge mess;
But all the time spent on it made me think twice,
After all, the puzzle was still a work in progress —
Maybe it was worthwhile to repair it, piece by piece.

My enthusiasm grew as the picture did steadily unfold,
For finishing it would truly be a great feat!
I quickly began filling up all the empty spaces,
Eagerly awaiting the time when it'd be finally complete —
Indeed, it was coming together, piece by piece.

And as the puzzle was coming to an end,
I marvelled at how the pieces had once seemed discrete;
And although there was a missing piece,
It somehow made the picture more significant and complete,
For 'twas a reminder that it was created piece by piece.

And as I looked at every piece, I began to see,
That alone they were quite plain and insignificant;
But when they all were closely joined together —
A beautiful picture they did represent:
True, a wonder is created piece by piece.

And so, life may sometimes seem like a perplexing puzzle,
We may find ourselves wondering why some things happen;
But like each piece, everything indeed has a purpose,
Together they'll form a beautiful picture in the end —
And time will reveal that to us, piece by piece.

3. Look Up to the Sky

Look up to the sky — so blue and clear,
Bathed in the glory of the sun's bright light;
'Twill fill your mind with joy and delight,
When there isn't a single dark cloud in sight.

Look up to the sky — see the little white clouds,
And let your imagination run fully wild;
As you watch the clouds take on various forms,
That dreamy white land will surely make you smile.

Look up to the sky when you're feeling down,
When storm clouds gather and overwhelm you;
Take heart, for it's not going to last forever,
The storm will pass and the sun will shine through.

Look up to the sky, as the rain slowly ceases,
And behold the rainbow, so glorious and magical;
Maybe braving the storm was worth it in the end —
For a wonder emerged from a scene once dismal.

Look up to the sky — as the sun sinks low,
As daylight fades and the sky seems aglow;
Then quickly it's all gone and darkness reigns —
But you know the sun will come out tomorrow.

Look up to the sky in the stillness of the night,
At the mystical moon and the twinkling stars
That during the day were veiled by the light,
For stars shine bright only when it's dark.

Look up to the sky — say a little prayer,
Be thankful and think of those you love;
Pour out your heart, for there is Someone who cares,
Who listens and watches o'er you from above.

Look up to the sky wherever you are,
'Twill give you courage and fill you with hope;
Look up and believe, and reach for your dreams,
For like the sky, they too have an endless scope.

Look up to the sky — as a new day dawns,
Breathe in the fresh air and calmly watch the sun rise;
And during the busy day, whenever you feel lost,
Just pause to take a little moment, and look up to the sky.

4. A Little Walk Down Memory Lane

Sometimes you really need to take
A little walk down memory lane,
Remember those blissful bygone days,
And think about them, once again.

And as you start to walk that path,
You'll find some sights that make you smile;
Those lovely meadows — so green and bright,
That make you stay there for a little while.

And slowly as you start to wander,
You hesitate to visit that valley yonder;
For a minute or two, you stop and ponder,
On how far you've come — 'tis truly a wonder!

You think of those dreary times,
When failure at you was thrown;
Thankful that you didn't give up hope,
And took defeat as a stepping stone.

For that wearying climb out that valley
Gave you strength to scale the lofty mountains,
It gave you courage to stand brave and tall,
Oh! What a happy time it was back then!

And as you continue your dreamy stroll,
You think of those who helped you on the way:
The people who helped you shine and grow,
And made you who you are today.

But your joy dims as you see grey stones,
A reminder of those who have gone before;
You pause, as the tears fill your eyes,
Sad, for they are not with you anymore.

As you think of the times spent with them,
You wish that they were somehow still here;
But maybe holding on to these few memories,
Will make them feel more near and dear.

Moving on, you start to think about how
These memories seem to keep you founded;
For even when the thunder roars and crashes,
You still can stand strong — firmly grounded.

And as your walk begins to come to an end,
You're glad for the wonderful memories you had;
Looking forward to the coming days,
And the exciting memories they may add.

Before you open your eyes, you take a last look,
At the past, now a calm and comforting scene;
Thinking about how perfectly imperfect,
This long journey of life so far has been.

Coming to the present, you open your eyes,
And gaze at the unknown path you haven't tread;
'Twill not be easy, but you can still smile —
For you'll make new memories, whatever lies ahead.

And then, maybe someday, by and by,
When you feel like rambling, once again;
You may once more wander in your mind,
And take another walk down memory lane.

TOGETHER WE CAN

5. Our One and Only Planet

Our beloved earth is facing grave danger,
This hurtful truth one can't deny.
The seasons strange, the sudden climate change,
And by now, you may wonder why?

Our industries and our dear appliances
Release greenhouse gases at a rate so alarming.
The burning of fuels and cutting of trees
Are all major causes of disastrous global warming.

The melting of ice, the rise in the sea,
The increase in earthquakes, floods and droughts,
Tornadoes and hurricanes, disappearances of islands,
'Tis really a catastrophe, beyond any doubt.

Come on! We must save our one and only planet,
Let's reduce the use of fuels, and plant more trees.
May our children never see a dilapidated world,
But happily live in a beautiful earth with ease.

6. Trees

Once upon a time, trees filled the scene
Trees standing tall with leaves so green
But one sad day, they were all cut down,
By selfish humans who only cared for a town.

As buildings were built, and humans began to stay,
The once clean air was polluted and grey,
Sickness increased, the surroundings were bleak,
And all because there wasn't a single tree.

Now one little child who moved to town,
Saw the devastation as he looked around,
He decided to be a change for the world to see,
And it all began by planting one little tree.

And the tree grew, and stood green and tall,
And its many seeds around did fall;
The once bleak land was all fresh and green,
Just because a little child planted a single tree.

The air become fresh, and there was more health,
For trees are truly a priceless wealth.
In the world today, as trees are ruthlessly cut down,
Can we make a change, and plant a tree in the ground?

The future is ours, but will it be a beautiful scene?
Will our planet once more be clean and green?
It all starts with us, with you and me,
Come, let us join hands, and plant more trees.

7. True Democracy

India – our beautiful and beloved country,
Don't we often wonder what its future might be?
Will we overcome all the struggles we face,
And when will we be a true democracy?

With all the challenges that we face each day:
Ignorance, disease, misery and poverty,
Will there be a day when all tears will be wiped away,
Oh , when will we be a true democracy?

There still are chains that we must loose,
The chains of discrimination, corruption and evil;
Can we loose them all and truly be free?
Oh when will we be a true democracy?

The answer lies in the hands of each one,
Each citizen that is a part of this vast country,
We must unite, for together we can,
Will the future unfold a true democracy?

The future is ours, and responsible we must be,
Lift up the poor, and those in need;
May we wholeheartedly serve our beloved country,
And together may we fulfil the dream of a true democracy.

8. Together We Can

A new decade dawned – 2020,
People's hopes and dreams were plenty:
Selfish, and only bothered about travel and money,
Not concerned at all about nature or family.

'Twas time for a drastic change,
So a microscopic virus took the stage;
In a short while, there was a global lockdown:
Offices, schools and factories were shut down.

The virus swiftly spread from place to place,
'Stay home, stay safe' became a common phrase.
And we all slowly realised the importance of family,
And began to rethink and set right our priorities.

Nature's beauty once more began to spring,
Without honking cars, birds began to sing;
Factories were closed, the air became clean,
And the ozone layer began to heal.

While we stayed home, we reflected back,
And marvelled that a virus had set us back on track;
Though this virus our dreams did shatter,
It showed us what truly mattered.

We learnt to care for each other: united we stand,
Whatever comes our way, together we can!
With priorities set right, at the future we gaze,
With one accord, hoping for better, brighter days.

9. COVID-19

As a new decade dawned – 2020,
People dreamed with aspirations a plenty;
Selfish and not caring for others a trifle,
They least expected my silent arrival.

As I looked at all these pompous human beings,
I decided it was time for a rude awakening;
So in the city of Wuhan, in China, I emerged,
And in a little while, I rapidly surged.

These humans still in pride did flounce,
And the whistleblower did they denounce!
Meanwhile, the scientists discovered my gene,
And I was given a name – COVID-19.

It was not long before I swiftly spread,
And throughout the world humans did me dread;
For this unexpected outbreak they weren't prepared,
The nations of the world were perturbed and scared.

They panicked at me, for I really was deadly,
And caught them in my grip when they least were ready;

I , the microscopic virus, was now the conqueror,
The dreams for the new decade were all in a blur.

In Asia, America, Australia, Africa and Europe,
I ruthlessly attacked till there wasn't much hope.
However some experts found a way to stop me –
People were told to wash and keep hands germ free.

Nevertheless, an immense impact I did make,
And those in authority strict measures did take,
Factories, offices and schools were shut down,
And the world's economy did face a breakdown.

People no longer in freedom do roam,
And many a family is confined to their home;
They hope a cure will soon be found,
From their lips a prayer they sound.

There's isn't much time to overcome me, as it were,
Unless people aren't selfish and care for each other.
I think to myself – how long will this last?
Will I soon become a part of the past?

Will the story be told of me – a virus that conquered man?
Or will humans realise that together they surely can?
I might go on or soon be gone, is all I can say,
Will man's good come to the fore, and together will they?

ODES TO EXCEPTIONAL PEOPLE

10. Dear Teacher...

Dear teacher, just like a candle,
Burning to give us light;
Extinguishing yourself
To make our future bright.

'Gainst all the struggles and the pains,
Your passion makes you fight;
You patiently endure
Just to teach us what is right.

You do your best to make us learn,
And help us our goals attain;
Relentlessly our mistakes correct –
Truly, that's a lot of strain!

And your homes too – so much stress,
Yet you never complain.
Please take note, my dear teacher,
Your toil and effort is not in vain.

For all your dedication and the lessons
You do to us impart,
I want to thank you, my dear teacher,
From the bottom of my heart.

11. Mother

She patiently endured
Just to bring a child into this world;
And that helpless and defenceless baby,
She lovingly nurtured.

Through all the good and the bad,
She always is there
With words of wisdom and encouragement,
And of course, a prayer.

True, she reprimands at times,
But that's only because she loves;
She is a guiding light
In life's sea — rocky and rough.

She has really done so much,
That I can never repay,
The least I can do is thank her,
So I sincerely say —

"Thank you, dear mother,
For your love and tender care,
For your selfless sacrifice,
And for always being there."

12. A Forever Friend

I wish that I could find a friend,
Who'd be loyal and true forever,
Who'd always be there to brighten my day,
Whatever may be the weather.

And when I think I finally found
A friend who understands my heart,
I begin to dream and fancy about
How we may grow up but never apart.

But in today's spurious world,
Where nothing really lasts forever;
It's disheartening to perceive that
A 'strong' bond can so easily be severed.

It's hard to find that 'someone' –
Who's there in both joy and distress;
Someone who can be a support and solace,
A someone who is loyal and selfless.

At times it feels like no one cares,
And you don't know just whom to trust;

Afraid to venture into new friendships,
Worried that 'forever' may just crumble to dust.

That's when you realise — in a world like this,
There isn't much you can expect.
There is one, only one Forever Friend,
And there's no other friend who is so perfect.

A Friend you can always go to,
Be if dark nights, or bright sunny days;
A Friend who never will forsake you,
Who's with you every step of the way.

A Friend whose promises are true,
A Friend who'll never you betray;
Who loves and cares and listens to you,
And graciously takes your burdens away.

When everything around seems so uncertain,
This faithful Friend remains steadfast and sure;
Whatever the shadows and storms you may face,
You know with this Friend, you will be secure.

And as I look at how people just come and go,
I'm glad that I've found my Forever Friend —
The One who loves me, just as I am,
My Friend who'll be there for me till the very end.

13. A Tribute to My Grandma

'The Lord is my Shepherd',
These words to her so dear:
It gave her strength and courage,
And made her pathway clear.

With her Shepherd, she had no want:
He stilled her every fear,
He bore her through each trial,
And wiped away each tear.

He led her through green pastures,
And through the waters still;
She followed in His footsteps,
With complete faith in His will.

When she walked through the valley,
E'en through the shadow of death;
Even then, she feared no ill,
Trusting in the Giver of each breath.

She followed where her Shepherd led,
And cast on Him her every care,
Comforted by the Shepherd's staff,
Knowing that He is always there.

Assured that His goodness and mercy,
Would follow her all her days;
Fully relying on her Shepherd,
To guide her in all her ways.

There came a valley in her path,
She became ill and grew weak;
Her Shepherd was there all those years,
When with none else she could speak.

Oh! She longed for that day!
When she would her homeland see,
When there would be no more pain,
And she would with her Shepherd be.

And on one rainy evening,
When she was peacefully asleep,
The Shepherd lovingly and gently
Called home His dear sheep.

Now she dwells in the house
Of her Saviour, forevermore;
And we look forward to that day,
When we'll meet on the other shore.

14. Led by the Saviour, All the Way

A Tribute to a 100 year old Grandma who impacted my life

"All the way my Saviour leads me" —
'Twas her steadfast conviction through her 100 years;
For she wholly trusted in her Lord and Master,
Knowing that He was always near.

She trusted her life in her Master's Hand,
Believing that He always knew what was best,
Assured that her Shepherd would guide and provide,
For in Him was her haven of refuge and rest.

When life wasn't easy and the going was tough,
She cast on the Saviour her every care;
Whatever the hurdles that came in her path,
She took everything to the Lord in prayer.

She exemplified how to selflessly live for others,
For the little that she had, she cheerfully gave;
She always showed love, compassion and care,
Oh! Her love will always on our hearts be engraved!

And she was blessed with a marvellous memory,
For she never failed to wish people on their special days;
Thinking about and praying for each one by name,
She truly was a light that shone with a bright blaze!

Even in her last days, when she was old and weak,
She still sang the praises of her Redeemer and Friend;
Whose goodness and mercy had followed her all her days;
She testified of His faithfulness until the very end.

She longed to go and be with her Saviour forevermore,
And till that day she was so loving, gracious and kind;
She did all she could for Him before she went Home,
And touched many lives, leaving a lasting legacy behind.

Now she blissfully dwells in the House of her Lord,
Enjoying His presence, face to face forevermore.
We'll hold on to the fond memories of her wonderful life,
And look forward to the day we'll meet on the other shore.

POEMS FOR SPECIAL OCCASIONS

15. Independence Day

India – our beautiful and beloved country
Celebrates 75 years of being free;
A freedom so precious, with a story to tell,
A tribute to those who fought for you and me:

Once upon a time India was bound,
By the chains of an oppressive British rule;
When it was too much to bear, people revolted,
They fought against the bonds that were so cruel.

From the struggle were born leaders brave and true,
Mahatma Gandhi, Subhash Chandra Bose, Jawaharlal Nehru;
Bhagat Singh, Mandal Pandey, Chandrashekhar Azad,
And Dr. Rajendra Prasad, just to name a few.

There were so many movements launched for Swaraj,
The Non-Cooperation and Civil Disobedience,
The Salt March and Quit India Movement,
Many battled for freedom at their own expense.

And there are many unsung heroes, courageous and brave,
Who fought and even died, our country to save;
You see, freedom had a cost that was oh so great,
And as we look back, our hearts with pride do resonate.

And on this very special Independence Day,
We thank our heroes for their lives that for India they gave,
For the sacrifices wrought and the struggles fought,
We truly are grateful for the freedom we've got.

And now, inspired, as we gaze at the future that before us is
spread,
We know that we can face the challenges that lie on our path
ahead
So together, let us join hands and look up to the sky,
As we pledge to make India's flag always fly high!

16. Diwali – The Festival of Lights

We all eagerly wait
For the Festival of Lights,
When all the shimmer and the shine
Makes our country so very bright.

The candles and the lamps
The fireworks and the sparks
Symbolise the victory
Of light over dark.

The lights give us joy,
Our hope is renewed:
That evil is triumphed over,
The final victor is 'good'.

Let us ponder on our lives,
May there be no evil deep down in,
Let the 'Light of the World'
Overcome the real darkness within.

May our lives be like lights,
With love and kindness from our hearts;
So we can spread joy and happiness,
Even when we are far apart.

This Festival of Lights,
Let us all joyfully unite:
For together we can make
Our country truly bright.

17. Christmas – The Season of Hope and Joy

It's Christmas – that season of hope and joy,
With a message so wondrous and true:
For it shows the infinite love of an Almighty God,
Presented to mere mortals like me and you.

The creator of the heavens and earth stooped down,
To be humbly born: in a manger lowly laid;
The One who holds the world in the palm of His hand,
Came and dwelt among people that He had made.

He showed us God's boundless love and mercy,
When He died on the cross, paying the price for our sins,
And rose again, to give the free gift of eternal life
To those who accept Him as their Saviour within.

That's the message of Christmas, simple and true,
Of God's love and grace towards me and you;
May the beauty of this wondrous gift,
Fill your heart with peace, hope and joy anew.

As we remember the miraculous birth of Christ,
May you feel God's love reaching out to you;
May you have the faith to believe in Him,
And may my Saviour be your Saviour too.

18. Another Year

Another year is dawning
And we know not what is in store,
But just take a pause, and look back
At God's faithfulness heretofore.

E'en though the year wasn't easy,
Change and challenges we all went through,
Yet God was always there, fully in control,
A God who is ever faithful and true.

His steadfast love we experienced
Each and every day;
His grace that led and guided us
Every step of the way.

The past year might have been filled
With change, troubled times, and fear,
But remember, through it all
That God was always near.

As we step into the new year,
We do not know what it holds,
Just trust God, don't worry or fear
For He is in full control.

In the midst of all your problems,
You will find His perfect peace;
No matter where you are,
His grace and love will never cease.

This new year, don't forget
That God is always with you,
Thus far He has led you
And He'll lead you through!

SHORT SNIPPETS

19. Fear

My fear lies in my mind,
Of the future – undefined;
A certain dread of the unknown,
For I know not what it holds.

Anxiety needs to be bravely faced,
It takes faith, and also courage;
And I need not worry nor fear,
For I know that God is always near

20. Only One Short Life

Only one short life on earth,
For Christ may it be worth;
'Tis only by His grace,
That I make it through each day.

In God I fully trust,
For He knows what is the best;
And as I in Him believe,
May my sincere prayer be –

"Lord take this life of mine,
Use it, for 'tis only Thine;
I wholly on Thee depend,
May I be faithful to the end."

HYMNS – SONGS FROM THE HEART

21. God's Leading Hand

Trust in the Lord to guide thee,
Only have faith and believe;
He treads the pathway before thee,
And He'll thee never leave;
The future He hath planned,
And He doth hold thy hand.

The Lord doth go before thee
Just trust and on Him depend,
He'll never fail nor forsake thee,
He'll lead thee to the end.

The path is not always easy,
It may at times be rough;
God's mercy and love never ceases,
His grace is more than enough;
Thus far He has led you,
And He will lead you through.

22. God is in Control

All around there is no peace,
For the world is in turmoil, and tomorrow's uncertain;
But why should we lose faith, when we have a hope,
For our Lord has proven faithful, time and again.

Times like this will soon be past,
Just trust in the Lord as long as it lasts;
And rest in His promises, fully assured
That all will be well, for He's in control.

All around there is anxiety,
But we fully trust in God, and we never should fear;
For His eye is on the sparrow, and He cares for us,
We can have complete faith in Him, for He's always near.

All around hope is declining,
But relying on the Lord, we can have hope and peace;
For He is always with us, whatever betide,
He is our eternal refuge, His grace will not cease.

23. Trust and Abide

When we look around in these troubled times,
We see much anxiety that hope declines;
But our sovereign God has a purpose and plan,
And He truly holds the world in His hand.

In the shadow of Thy wings may we make our refuge
Till these calamities be over past;
Lord, help us to trust Thee whatever betide,
Through times like this, may we in Thee abide.

The Saviour who is always by our side,
Just bids us to trust and in Him abide;
For we can do nothing ourselves without Him,
Only He can give peace in times like this.

Abiding in Him we have nought to fear,
For nothing can harm us when He is near;
We can surely have faith and believe in His Word,
And rest in His promises, steadfast and sure.

A LITTLE ABOUT THE POET...

24. About Myself

In the land of the living for sixteen long years,
With a heart filled with memories it holds very dear.
As I look at myself, and who I am today,
I just wonder, take a pause, and look back down life's narrow
way.

The journey began on the 19ᵗʰ of September, 2005
A precious gift was born, the gift of a child.
My parents named me Jane – the gift of God,
For them, a child was truly a great reward.

I, a blank slate, on which my parents wrote everyday,
Priceless lessons that guide me all along the way,
They nurtured and developed my unique personality,
And gave me opportunities to have a speciality.

My family – the first people I ever met,
Who taught me values I can never forget.
They taught me to love, have faith and go on,
An anchor so strong in the fiercest of storms.

My sister – my first friend and foe,
Who helps me whenever I to her go;
We share secrets, have fun, fight and play,
She'll always be close to my heart, come what may.

And the time came, when I was around two,
When for the first time, I stepped into school.
I made new friends, learnt to read and to write,
'Twas truly a time filled with delight.

I learnt so many things which I never knew,
And discovered myself, and what I can do;
I also learnt the right from the wrong,
And with different people how to get along.

The path wasn't straight, it did take a turn
When my beloved father did leave this world;
But the path did not stop, it went on ahead,
And my Heavenly Father before me doth tread.

As I walked down the path, I discovered myself,
My talents, skills and weaknesses as well;
For I can be really adamant and impatient,
And I must work hard, my weaknesses to transcend.

I found I can be loving and kind too,
And I'm also honest, and loyal and true.
A 'sorry' is real, when my mistake I realise,
But oh! How hard it is to apologise.

I discovered my talents – playing the piano and violin,
And also came upon the hidden author and poet within,
And a little skill in drawing and photography;
I surely thank God for all He has given me.

And there are things that I enjoy to do,
Robotics and playing with nuts and with screws,
To quill and to knit and also to read,
I really must thank my parents, indeed!

I come to the present and then look ahead,
But I know not what before me is spread,
One thing I know, I onward must go,
And focus on my dreams and my goals.

In all I do, I'll strive to excel,
Never forgetting to be true to myself;
Doing my best with whatever I've got
And keeping in mind all I've been taught.

I thank the people in my life, wherever they are,
For helping me to come this far,
I also thank God for leading the way,
And bringing me to where I am today.

A bundle of character, talents and skills,
May all be used my dreams to fulfil,
I know I'm not in this world by chance,
For of course, God surely has His plans.

What they may be, I do not know
But trusting in God, I'll onward go;
For He is my Guide, my Master and Friend,
And He'll lead me safely through to the end.